Advent Lights

Advent Lights

A Journey through Advent with the Advent Wreath

Daily devotions for the busy season of Advent

Hannah Hoskin

To Julia

CONTENTS

INTRODUCTION

Although the calendar year is coming to an end, Advent marks the start of a new liturgical year in the church. The word Advent means the arrival of something new and important. For Christians this is a time of looking forward to the arrival of the most important gift; the birth of Jesus Christ, celebrated on Christmas Day.

Many church traditions mark the weeks leading up to Christmas through the lighting of candles on an Advent wreath, in which each of the five candles represents a theme in the story of the Christian faith. In this book, you are invited to pause and ponder the meaning of these stories through short daily reflections and prayers, as we are guided by the candles towards Christmas.

Each entry stands alone, and as Christmas falls on a different day of the week each year, it may be that you omit some of the readings for the Fourth Week of Advent.

You may also wish to light a candle each day, or make your own Advent wreath, as you follow these readings.

First Week of Advent

Advent Sunday

Churches and homes across the world mark the weeks of Advent through the lighting of an Advent wreath. Although there are various origins and interpretations, our modern Advent wreath comprises a circle of greenery, with four candles placed around the edge and one in the middle. Every Sunday during Advent another candle is lit, culminating in the lighting of the middle candle, which symbolises Christ, on Christmas Day.

The first candle, lit on Advent Sunday, represents the founders of the faith, known as the Patriarchs. Just as Christ's teaching drew on the lives of his ancestors, we are reminded to give thanks for those who have been significant in shaping our own lives. We reflect on our family and our role models, all those who have influenced and supported us.

The first candle is also associated with hope. Hope is what inspires people to go on, in challenging times as well as in times of anticipation. As we journey towards Christmas, the promise of Christ is a light in the darkness, a beacon of hope on our journey.

PRAYER

Heavenly Father, as we remember the founders of our faith, we give thanks for those who have influenced our lives. May we be mindful that our actions may shape the lives of future generations, and live accordingly. We thank you that in the darkest days, the promise of your Son gives us the hope of future joy, and life everlasting.

Amen

Monday - Keep Watch!

Mark 13: 35
Therefore, keep awake – for you do not know when the master of the house will come. *

Advent is a time when we look forward to celebrating the birth of Jesus Christ on Christmas Day. It can be a time of great anticipation; children waiting excitedly to open presents, long-awaited family gatherings, the wonderful Christmas music and carol services.   And yet, in the church year, Advent is also a time of reflection and penitence, looking to the *second* coming of Christ, at the end of time.

In an age where there is so much distraction, it can be difficult to find the space to reflect on whether we are ready to meet Jesus when he comes. Sometimes it can feel easier to put this to one side whilst we get on with the practicalities of preparing for Christmas. But if not now, then when? Taking time just to be still with God each day can benefit our minds as well as our souls, helping us to keep a hold on who we are amidst the busyness of life.   Viewed in this way, the whole month of Advent is a gift.

PRAYER

Heavenly Father, as we begin our Advent journey, help us to remember that you walk alongside us. May we take time today to just be still and know that you are God. As we prepare for Christ's coming at Christmas, may we also be ready for when he comes again.

Amen

*Read the full story here: Mark 13: 32-37

Tuesday - Unlikely Heroes

Luke 1: 54-55
He has helped his servant Israel, remembering to be merciful to Abraham and his descendants forever, just as he promised our ancestors. *

As Advent is the beginning of a new church year, it is fitting that we look back at God's early promises to his people. Abraham, Isaac, Jacob and David are the Patriarchs traditionally referred to during Advent, and their stories remind us that God can use unlikely candidates to bring about his kingdom. God's chosen people descend from an elderly Abraham and his barren wife Sarah. Jacob, father of the 12 Tribes of Israel, deviously cheats his elder brother Esau on several occasions. Even the great King David, who gave us such wonderful Psalms, was overtaken by moments of human weakness.

Nonetheless, these are the founders of the faith, used by God to prepare the way for Christ. We should be in no doubt, then, that he may just as easily use our weaknesses and imperfections, our unlikely situations, to further his kingdom.

PRAYER

Heavenly Father, we thank you for those who have paved the way for our faith today. We remember all who have had a direct influence on our lives, and pray that we in turn may inspire and encourage others. Help us to remember that, whatever our weakness, you can transform it into our strength, and use it to bring blessing to ourselves and others.

Amen

*Read Mary's Magnificat here: Luke 1: 46-55

Wednesday - Wrestling in the Darkness

Genesis 32: 24, 28
So Jacob was left alone and a man wrestled with him till daybreak... Then the man said, "Your name will no longer be Jacob, but Israel, because you have struggled with God and with humans and have overcome." *

As Jacob prepared to meet his estranged brother, Esau, he wrestled all night with an unnamed man, whom we understand to be an angel of God, or even God himself. At the end of this encounter the man touched Jacob's hip, dislocating it and leaving him with a permanent physical reminder of his struggle. But in response to his perseverance, Jacob also received the man's blessing, along with a new name and destiny.

In truth, we all wrestle with our faith, or God, at some time in our lives. Maybe, like Jacob, it is because we are carrying the burden of past indiscretions, and are partly wrestling with ourselves. Maybe we are experiencing what St John of the Cross called 'the dark night of the soul'. Yet God gives us the space to work through our doubts and fears. And when we have wrestled enough, he gently touches us, to acknowledge his presence, and our lives are changed forever.

PRAYER

Heavenly Father, sometimes the mountain before us seems impossible to climb, and the doubts within us too powerful to overcome. When we grow tired, ease our burdens. May we always remember that we will never be tested beyond the limit of our endurance.

Amen

*Read the full story here: Genesis 32: 22-30

Thursday - Nothing is Impossible with God

Genesis 18: 13-14
Then the Lord said to Abraham, "Why did Sarah laugh and say, 'Will I really have a child, now that I am old?' Is anything too hard for the Lord?" *

Abraham's wife, Sarah, was well past child-bearing age, but the Lord appeared to Abraham and promised them a child. When she overheard this, Sarah laughed in disbelief for, like us, Sarah could only see the physical, human limitations standing in the way of such a promise. She needed to be reminded that nothing is impossible with God.

Few of us may receive a dramatic miracle in our own lives. Yet God can transform even the most hopeless situation into something beyond our imagining. Just like Sarah, the outcome may not be the one we desire or expect at the time, so we have to have faith that God knows us better than we know ourselves. We may never know the future legacy of our own transformed lives.

PRAYER

Heavenly Father, help us to remember that nothing is impossible with you. When our paths take an unexpected turn, give us vision to see what new thing you are bringing about in our lives. Transform us into who we are meant to be, through your grace.

Amen

*Read the full story here: Genesis 18: 1-15

Friday - Hope

Romans 8: 24-25
Who hopes for what they already have? But if we hope for what we do not yet have, we wait for it patiently.

The lead-up to Christmas can be a busy time, with many distractions, and it can be a time when we feel the absence of loved-ones the most. But during Advent, we do not just wait in the darkness. We wait with hope.

Unlike a child hoping to receive a particular Christmas present, but knowing that it is probably out of their reach, we can be assured that what we hope for will surely come. For we are not just waiting for Christmas Day, but for the day when Jesus comes again, and everything is made new. We may not know the day or hour, indeed, it may not even be in our own lifetime. But if we have faith, then we always have hope.

PRAYER

Heavenly Father, lighten our darkness, that we may walk boldly with hope. Reassure us when we have doubts, and remind us of your promises. Help us to bring hope to others, and to look forward to your coming.
Amen

Saturday - Quiet Prayer

Hebrews 6: 19
We have this hope as an anchor for the soul, firm and secure.

Set aside a moment of quiet today, and allow your mind to dwell on the ever-present God.
Reassure yourself that, whatever insecurities you are feeling at the moment, God is your anchor.
Allow yourself to lean on him.

Second Week of Advent

Second Sunday of Advent

In many Anglican churches three of the candles in the Advent wreath are purple, with rose pink for the third Sunday. Purple is the liturgical colour for Advent, and represents penitence, which is why many churches do not have flowers or decorations during this period. This makes it all the more special when all the candles are lit and the church is beautifully adorned on Christmas Day.

The second candle on our Advent wreath represents the Prophets, who foretold the coming of the Messiah. We are reminded that God has a greater plan, and that we can look forward, not just to Christmas, but to eternal life through Christ's saving grace.

The second candle is also associated with peace. Amid the busy rush of Christmas preparations, it can be a reminder to seek out time for quiet reflection during Advent.

PRAYER

Heavenly Father, may the stories of the Prophets teach us patience to wait for your timing. Help us to remember that for everything there is a time of preparation and a time of fulfilment. May we connect with you through moments of quiet during this Advent season, and find a deep sense of your peace.

Amen

Monday – Enjoy the Journey

2 Peter 3: 13
But in keeping with his promise we are looking forward to a new heaven and a new earth, where righteousness dwells.

December can feel like a period of preparation, leading up to the big day; decorating the home, writing cards, wrapping presents, preparing food. As Christians, our whole lives might feel this way too, as we prepare and wait for the coming of Christ on the last day. Of course, we must prepare and we must look forward. But we should also remember to enjoy the journey. To enjoy the Christmas preparations, to take pleasure in the wrapping of the presents. In other words, recognising that the means should be as valued as the end.

As we wait for the coming of a new and perfect earth, we must remember to enjoy the wonders of *this* world, which is a beautiful reflection of what is to come.

PRAYER

Heavenly Father, help us to keep a child-like sense of wonder as we prepare for Christmas. As we look forward to what is to come, help us to take pleasure in what we have now. Inspire us to enjoy the journey with you, knowing that by doing so, we are doing our part in bringing about your Kingdom.

Amen

Tuesday – Wilderness

Isaiah 40: 3
A voice of one calling: "In the wilderness, prepare the way for the Lord; make straight in the desert a highway for our God."*

Just as the prophets foretold the coming of the Messiah, we have been looking for the return of Christ for millennia. This Old Testament reading, which is referenced in all four gospels, is usually related to John the Baptist. However, it can also be interpreted as a call to all people, to bring the good news to our own wilderness places. These can be places in the world around us, but equally those dry, wilderness places within our own hearts.

The Old Testament prophets did not have an easy life, often speaking against the status quo, and may themselves have felt that they were 'in the wilderness'. Yet they held firm to the truth when they were mocked, despised, even facing death. There are those who still risk their lives to spread the good news in inhospitable places today.

PRAYER

Heavenly Father, there are so many wilderness places needing the touch of your love. Open our eyes to see them, give us the courage to proclaim your saving grace, and help us not to neglect the wilderness places within our own hearts. Lord, come and fill them with your presence.

Amen

*Read the full story here: Isaiah 40: 1-5

Wednesday – Send Me!

Isaiah 6: 8
Then I heard the voice of the Lord saying, "Whom shall I send? And who will go for us?" And I said, "Here am I. Send me!" *

Isaiah, the most frequently quoted prophet from the Old Testament, was chosen by God to see a wonderful vision of heaven. He felt unworthy to bear witness to such a sight, but angels touched his lips with a fiery coal, making them 'clean' to proclaim what he had seen. This emboldened him to say with confidence 'Send me!'.

It is easy to feel daunted, even unworthy, when we feel God calling us to something new. He may prompt us to take paths we never dreamed we would tread. Equally we may be called back in a direction where we have previously failed. Either way, these things may tug at our hearts, whilst we try our hardest to ignore them. At these times, we should take courage from the story of Isaiah, and remember that each one of us is chosen by God for something unique to us. Just as Isaiah's lips were made ready by the burning coal, God will equip us for the work he calls us to do.

PRAYER

Heavenly Father, help us to always keep an ear open to your calling. Grant us the courage of Isaiah to say "Here am I. Send me!" Touch our lips with the fire of your love, that you may speak through our words and actions in whatever task you call us to do.

Amen

*Read the full story here: Isaiah 6: 1-8

Thursday – Plans

Jeremiah 29: 11-12
"For I know the plans I have for you," declares the Lord, "plans to prosper you and not to harm you, plans to give you hope and a future. Then you will call on me and come and pray to me, and I will listen to you."

These words, recorded by the prophet Jeremiah, have inspired and encouraged Christians throughout the ages. Society dictates that we make plans in life; in our careers, our relationships and our leisure activities. We may be encouraged to take control of our own destiny, but what about the plans which God has for us? As scripture tells us, God knows us better than we know ourselves and what's more, he will listen to our desires and requests when we pray to him. Life can take unexpected turns, not all of them good. But if we trust in God, knowing that he has a plan for us, we can be reassured that things will work out for the best, even if it doesn't seem that way at the time.

PRAYER

Heavenly Father, we often fill our minds with unnecessary worries about the future. Help us to recognise the signposts you plant before us, and to allow your plans for us to develop as we travel through life. Lord, hear us and guide us.

Amen

Friday — Peace

John 14: 27
Peace I leave with you; my peace I give you. I do not give to you as the world gives. Do not let your hearts be troubled and do not be afraid.

Although it may be viewed as something benign, peace holds more power than any act of aggression. Imagine what a different place the world would be if everyone lived in peace! It is a catalyst for well-being.

As well as the more wide-reaching peace between nations and individuals, we should also strive for peace within ourselves. It is through finding inner peace that we can inspire others to do the same, with consequences we might never imagine.

We all find peace for our souls in different ways; time alone, time with loved ones, time in the natural world. These can also be times in which we connect with God, who promises a deep peace, through Jesus. The peace of a child asleep in its mother's arms; safe, secure, loved.

PRAYER

Heavenly Father, when our lives are busy, help us to make time to be quiet and at peace with you. Restore our souls with the peace which only you can give. May it radiate from us to bring calm to those around us.

Amen

Saturday – Quiet Prayer

Matthew 5: 9
Blessed are the peacemakers, for they will be called children of
God.

Set aside a moment of quiet today to pray for places in the
world that cry out for peace.
Ask God to show you the areas of inner conflict in your own
life which are in need of his peace.
Allow the peace of God to wash over you, and allow yourself
to be transformed by the renewing power of his peace.

Third Week of Advent

Third Sunday of Advent

Symbolism is an important part of tradition, and can bring deeper meaning to our devotions. The Advent wreath is usually in the shape of a circle, a symbol of God's love which has no beginning or end. The evergreen foliage, with which it is traditionally decorated, symbolises eternal life.

The third candle on the Advent wreath represents John the Baptist, who prepared the way for Christ's ministry. John was not afraid to stand up for what he believed in, and we remember those who have had the courage to stand up for their faith throughout the ages.

The third candle is also associated with joy, and this Sunday is widely known as 'Gaudete' Sunday (meaning 'Rejoice'). Rather like Mothering Sunday during Lent, this is traditionally a more joyful Sunday during the penitent season of Advent. The busy lead-up to Christmas can sometimes be a time of anxiety rather than joy, and this Sunday is an opportunity to re-engage with the joyful news of Christ's coming.

PRAYER

Heavenly Father, we thank you that each one of us can play a part in preparing for the coming of your kingdom. Inspired by John the Baptist, may we have the courage to stand up for our faith. As we look forward to Christmas, may our lives bear witness to the good news, bringing joy into the lives of those around us.

Amen

Monday – Renewal

Matthew 11: 28
Come to me, all you who are weary and burdened, and I will
give you rest.

Historically, Advent was kept as a period of fasting and
abstinence. Gaudete Sunday allowed a day of respite from these
observances, in the hope that believers would be refreshed and
sustained to continue with their devotions.
Today most Christians do not keep Advent with such strictness.
However, we can still benefit from a time of rest and renewal,
if not from strict routines, then from overloading our lives with
unrealistic expectations and commitments. It is healthy to
acknowledge when we need to step back, and when we need to
push on. This week is a good opportunity to reflect on where
we are, and to allow ourselves some time to be thankful for all
the blessings in our lives.

PRAYER

Heavenly Father, when we are hard on ourselves, remind us of your great mercy. Help us to know that we can come to you for rest and renewal, as Jesus promised us. Refresh us at this mid-point in Advent, and strengthen us to continue walking with you towards Christmas joy.

Amen

Tuesday – Supporting Act

Luke 1: 36-37
"Even Elizabeth your relative…is going to have a child in her old age. For nothing is impossible with God." *

Beautifully echoing the story of Abraham and Sarah, John the Baptist was also born to parents who were long past child-bearing age. This time, it was John's father, Zechariah, who questioned the messenger of this news, causing the angel to render him literally speechless until John was born and named! John is often called 'the forerunner', which evokes a powerful image of a torch-bearer lighting the way for those following behind. He paves the way for Jesus and, in a wonderful paradox, it is John who baptises Christ at the start of his earthly ministry.

Sometimes we may be called to prepare the way for something to come, something which we may never even see. We should never underestimate this role or see ourselves as insignificant. It is only because of the foundations that the house is able to stand.

PRAYER

Heavenly Father, grant us humility to recognise when we are to play a supporting role, and never to undervalue its importance. Give us confidence in our abilities when we are called to your work, however unlikely that calling may seem. Equip us for the task, and help us not to be diverted by seeking recognition or reward.

Amen

*Read the full story here: Luke 1: 5-25

Wednesday – Set Apart

Luke 1: 15
"For he will be great in the sight of the Lord. He is never to take wine or other fermented drink, and he will be filled with the Holy Spirit even before he is born."

John the Baptist lived no ordinary life. Gabriel's prophecy, and John's way of life, suggest that he was a Nazirite, someone whose outward actions were an expression of a vow to be holy. His life was set apart for God.

There are many outward signs that a person has dedicated their life to God. For example, through the ages, nuns, monks and many priests have chosen not to marry, as a sign that they are committed to God alone. We are not all called to live this way. However, if we choose to follow Christ, we choose to live differently, and this should be evident to those around us. What are the visible signs in *our* lives which show the world that we have chosen to be set apart for God?

PRAYER

Heavenly Father, by the baptism of water and the Holy Spirit we are made new. May our lives reflect that we are set apart for you, through the way in which we choose to live. Give us courage when others question our choices, and make our path ever clear to us.

Amen

Thursday – Lanterns

John 1: 8
He himself was not the light, but he came to testify to the light.

The famous chorus *Jesus bids us Shine* tells a simple truth about the Christian faith; the presence of the living God should shine out through us in our words and actions. However, like John the Baptist, we ourselves are not the light, nor does God ask us to be. We are like lanterns containing the holy fire. Just as the lantern glass needs to be clean in order to give out the most light, we must endeavour to keep our lives free from those things which can hide the light within.

This might seem like a huge undertaking, but we are not left to struggle alone. We have a Saviour who forgives us when life gets messy, and washes us clean again and again. For it is when the light of Christ is able to shine brightly in us, that we are our best and most beautiful selves.

PRAYER

Heavenly Father, burn brightly within us, so that your love and power can be seen at work in our lives. When we feel dulled by sin, gently restore us back to brightness. May your light within us illuminate our path, revealing the way for us, and for those we meet on our journey.
Amen

Friday – Joy

Philippians 4: 4
Rejoice in the Lord always. I will say it again: Rejoice!

John the Baptist leapt for joy in his mother's womb when she greeted her cousin Mary, who was carrying the Christ child within her. What a wonderful image, and a reminder that all living things can meet the Lord with joy!

There are as many ways to express joy as there are different people, and we need to be mindful to express joy in our own way for it to be sincere. There can be moments when we just cannot contain it within ourselves, and it is there for all to see. The same joy can be felt quietly, and internally. What is important is that we find a way to connect with joy in our faith, and in our lives. It is an essential element of our being, and if we believe in God's promises, how can we not rejoice?

PRAYER

Heavenly Father, we thank you for the gift of joy. In all the varied experiences of life, help us to find reasons for joyfulness, however small. Refresh our hearts as Christmas draws nearer, and help us to find lasting joy in the time we spend with one another, and with you.

Amen

Saturday - Quiet Prayer

Nehemiah 8: 10
The joy of the Lord is your strength.

Set aside a moment of quiet today and call to mind a moment
which gave you deep joy.
It may be recent, or it may feel like it has been some time since
you experienced joy in your life. Either way, recall that feeling,
let it bring a smile to your face, and thank God for it.
Let that feeling of joy strengthen you as you go into your day.

Fourth Week of Advent

Fourth Sunday of Advent

Two evergreen plants traditionally used to decorate the Advent wreath are holly and ivy. The spiky leaves of the holly are a symbol of Christ's crown of thorns, a reminder of what is to come. By contrast, the flowing leaves of ivy, considered as a feminine plant, symbolise Christ's mother Mary.

The fourth candle on the Advent wreath represents the Virgin Mary, who carried the Christ child in her womb, and held him in her arms. With Mary, we contemplate a mystery so beautifully expressed in the words of the poet Giles Fletcher; *See how small room my infant Lord doth take, whom all the world is not enough to hold.* *

The fourth candle is also associated with love. As we ponder the cosmic significance of the coming of Christ we should never forget that, at the very heart of it, is love; God's love for us, God's love through us. When everything is stripped away, love remains, and love triumphs.

PRAYER

Heavenly Father, we marvel that your coming to earth hinged upon the faith of a young girl. Grant us that same faith and willingness to trust in you, knowing that with God, anything is possible. May our lives be illuminated by love for you and for others.

Amen

Christ's Victory and Triumph, Giles Fletcher (1610)

Monday – Saying 'Yes'

Luke 1: 38
"I am the Lord's servant," Mary answered. "May your word to me be fulfilled."

Would Mary have said 'yes' if she had known what sorrow was to come, or understood the enormity of what she was part of? If we had been in Mary's place, would we have said 'yes'? We cannot know the answer to these questions. But the bible tells us that Mary trusted in God so fully that she agreed to step into the unknown. It was enough for her to start the journey in faith, knowing that the Lord would be with her, whatever may come. It would be a journey of great joys, and equally great sorrows, and a sword would pierce her soul.

There may be times when we are called to a new path, and fear to take the first step. Like Mary, we need to have confidence to say 'yes', and leave the rest to God.

PRAYER

Heavenly Father, when the road ahead seems daunting, help us to go forward in faith, trusting that our future is in your hands. Give us confidence to say 'yes' to the new directions in which you lead us. May the angel's greeting to Mary also reassure us; 'the Lord is with you'.

Amen

Tuesday – Treasure in the Heart

Luke 2: 19
But Mary treasured up all these things and pondered them in her heart.

At a time of year when the retail industry is at its peak, it is easy to focus on material gifts, food and social pleasures. These things all have their place, but they should not overshadow the 'treasures of the heart'. As Jesus' mother, Mary's life brought events which she maybe did not understand at the time, such as the extraordinary visitors and the prophesies spoken over her infant son. Yet she knew that these things were special, and treasured them in her heart. Later on, the truths would become clear to her, but until such a time, she was content to hold them as precious, where no-one could take them away.
Amid the busyness of Christmas, we would do well to follow the example of Mary; to step back, treasure the truths of the Christmas story and ponder them in our hearts. For 'where your treasure is, there your heart will be also.' (Matthew 6:21)

PRAYER

Heavenly Father, help us to discern what is important and precious in our lives, and to treasure these things in our hearts. Like Mary, may we take time to ponder the meaning of your truths. May these treasures enrich our relationships with you and with each other.

Amen

Wednesday – Nothing is Impossible with God

Luke 1: 34-35,37-38
"How will this be," Mary asked the angel, "since I am a virgin?"
The angel answered, "The Holy Spirit will come upon you, and
the power of the Most High will overshadow you. So the holy
one to be born will be called the Son of God. For no word
from God will ever fail."

Echoing the angel's message to Sarah in the first week of
Advent, we once again hear that nothing is impossible with
God. This time, the receiver of the message does not laugh,
but expresses unquestioning faith in God. If we go beyond the
familiar story and look at what is really happening here, we are
reminded how hugely profound this moment is; God makes
himself incarnate in the womb of an ordinary human woman.
That really does seem like the impossible!
Although our own experiences may seem to pale in
comparison, the truth remains that God uses us, just as we are,
to bring about his purposes. Even if what he has planned seems
impossible to our human comprehension.

PRAYER

Heavenly Father, help us never to doubt that all things are possible with you. When the way ahead seems unlikely, give us the confidence to keep moving forward. Grant us faith to put our hand in yours, Lord, and walk the path you have set before us.

Amen

Thursday – One Family in Christ

Mark 3: 33-34

"Who are my mother and my brothers?" he asked. Then he looked at those seated in a circle round him and said, "Here are my mother and brothers!" *

Christmas in the West has become regarded as a time to be with family. The Christmas message of love naturally prompts us to want to be with those whom we are closest to, but this can make it a difficult time for those who have no family, or are separated from loved-ones.

It must have been hard for Mary to hear Jesus making no distinction between his closest family and those gathered around him, who may only have met Jesus that day. But he was making an important statement about the family of God; all are equal, all are included, all are family.

We should treasure and include all God's family, as all are equally precious in his sight. This is not always easy, as we find some people harder to love than others – even family. At this time of year, it is worth making a mental note of those who might benefit from being included – not just at Christmas, but all year round. When Jesus, on the cross, entrusted the care of his mother Mary to his disciple John, he was doing exactly that.

PRAYER

Heavenly Father, although you understand that we love some people more than others, help us to re-imagine the definition of family. Open our hearts to others, and help us to see them as you see them. Lead us towards those whom you would entrust to our care.

Amen

*Read the full story here: Mark 3: 31-35

Friday – Love Came Down at Christmas

1 John 4: 19
We love because he first loved us.

In the original Greek of the New Testament there are many words to describe the different types of love. As we learn to love and to be loved, we discover the practical, as well as the emotional ways that love can manifest itself, including, as Jesus demonstrated so powerfully, sacrificial love.

If God's gift to us was a physical present, just like those presents under the tree, love would be the wrapping and love would be the contents. Our response to this gift, according to Jesus' commandments, is to love God and to love one another. Simple, yet so very complex. But the God who makes himself vulnerable in the form of a tiny baby sets an example for us to follow; love can be costly, but it is the most wonderful gift we can ever give or receive. In any act of love, God is present.

PRAYER

Heavenly Father, we thank you for the many expressions of love which you have set within our hearts. May our giving and receiving of love be magnified this Christmas time, in acts both large and small. Show us where love is needed, and fill our hearts so that we have an abundance of love to share.

Amen

Saturday – Quiet Prayer

John 3: 16
For God so loved the world that he gave his one and only Son,
that whoever believes in him shall not perish but have eternal
life.

Set aside a moment of quiet today, and ponder God's
remarkable gift.
Treasure this in your heart, and carry it with you into your
Christmas celebrations.

Christmas Day

Christmas Day

John 1: 1-5

In the beginning was the Word, and the Word was with God, and the Word was God. He was with God in the beginning. Through him all things were made; without him nothing was made that has been made. In him was life, and that life was the light of all mankind. The light shines in the darkness, and the darkness has not overcome it.

The waiting is over, the Advent of Christ is upon us! On Christmas Day, the fifth candle is lit, to represent Jesus Christ, the light of the world.

This candle sits in the centre of the wreath, as Christ is at the centre of all things. Around him sit the four candles which represent those whose lives have been illuminated by his presence. Perhaps we can imagine ourselves as one of those candles, looking up to Christ and receiving his light.

As we reflect on our Advent journey, let us go into this day prepared to meet the Christ child; the one who was, and is, and is to come. This Christmas Day may we, like Mary, treasure up in our hearts the light which no darkness can ever overcome.

PRAYER

As we reflect on the fully illuminated Advent wreath:

Heavenly Father, we give you thanks for this season of Advent, and for the chance to reflect upon our faith. Help us to take hope, peace and joy into the world throughout the year. Just as Mary made space for you, may we always make space for you in our lives. And may love be the greatest gift which we receive and give to others, this Christmastide and always.

Amen

Printed in Great Britain
by Amazon